Bar Stool Poet

Bar Stool Poet

by

Marv Ward

Wateree Creek Creations
Chapin, SC

Bar Stool Poet. Copyright 2023 by Marv Ward. All rights reserved. Printed in the United States of America. No part of this book may be used or reproduced in any manner whatsoever without written permission except in the case of brief quotations embodied in critical articles or reviews. For information please contact Wateree Creek Creations, an imprint of Muddy Ford Press, LLC, 1009 Muddy Ford Road, Chapin, SC 29036.

Wateree Creek Creations
is an imprint of
MuddyFordPress.com

Library of Congress Control Number: 2023946215
ISBN: 978-1-942081-38-8

Table of Contents

Bar Stool Poet 5

Splattered Fantasies 6

A Letter to The Artist 7

Fear 8

The Dealer 10

The Late Bloomer 12

Corona 13

The Warm Light of Normalcy 14

The Wren 16

The Wilted Rose 17

Living 18

Wonder Why 19

The Night of the Pearl 21

Belle Star 29

Carolina Lady 30

Genesis 31

Disco Nights 34

Don Pablo's 35

Desire 36

Five Points 37

Grass 38

Java Jive 39

Tuning Up 40

Sittin' In 41

Christmas With Harry 42

The Time Before Knowing 44

Under the Watchful Eye of Venus 46

Sojourners 47

The Chosen Ones? 48

Free Tickets 49

Spirits of Samhain 51

Road Dreams 52

Morning Prayer 53

Driving Through Georgia 54

Seven 55

Perspective 56

Politic 58

Priorities 59

Lady Bug 61

Hazelnut Dream 63

Diver 64

Rebirth 65

Fine Art 66

Missing You 67

The Wait 68

Just Because 69

Rainbow Time 70

Love 71

Beyond Shangri-La 72

Alone Together 73

Bar Stool Poet

I did not attend university.
I am not schooled in literary arts.
I am a bar stool poet,
profanely pontificating on paper
what the muse whispers in my ear.
Delighting in the delirium of misconstrued structure,
missing punctuation
and irreverent entendre.
So, there is no why,
no how,
no process,
simply words, wine and whimsy;
therapy in a maddened existence.
I am a bar stool poet
There is no explanation
only observations.
Salvation seeking in a sea of mixed drink emotions
sobering thoughts
sometimes
unabashed inner visions
without a syllabus or translation
I am a bar stool poet,
I just write.

Splattered Fantasies

      Air, heavy
enough to cut with a knife.
Somewhere between
      the wilted flowers
          and the sad
mouthed gardener
I sit,
      watching
          the laughing
childern.
Scattered pages,
      splattered fantasies,
          the brush
misses the canvas.
I throw away the canvas,
      and frame the floor.

A Letter To The Artist

Painter, paint me a day,
filled with the laughter of children,
bubbling with sunshine and love
a rainbow above
and cold white castle dreams
that melt into oceans.

Painter, paint me a night,
streaked with the lights of desire,
black as a hidden meaning
stars gleaming
with a shadow moon
to bathe and wash the soul.

Painter, paint me a life,
born in the joy of worship,
raised in the pain of heartbreak,
aged with mistake,
alive with every color of emotion
the mind can bear.

Painter, paint for me please.

Fear

I must admit, I fear many things,
foremost the loss of love.
A unique treasure,
once found,
leaves an abysmal chasm
marked by scars and tears when it is gone.
I cower when encountering reptiles.
Childhood trauma
has left a gaping hole in my soul
from unexpected meetings.
And, the ever present unknown of death.
I have never believed in blind faith,
trusting my senses and confidence
of feeling to reveal the truth of being.
But now, when faced with the looming reality,
the darkness of doubt holds more terror,
than I have ever experienced.
But I refuse to be overcome
with dread,
or doubt,
and adamantly deny it the chance
to interfere with living,
or to blot the beauty of existence
from my eyes.
Being a "Boomer"
FDR's words of wisdom resound in my heart
and I will not fear, fear.
I will strive to persevere,

rise above
embrace the light of life
let peace fill my soul
and live unafraid.

The Dealer

It's easy to have a love hate
relationship with a drug pusher

    when love is the drug.

    You want it,

        you need it

            you'll do
            anything to get it

even though you know the
ordeal is driving you insane,

    and your demise is the
result of the pursuit.

But as you lay transfixed in the
arms of your dealer,

    you are willing to pay any price

        to envelop your
        being in this sensation.

And when it is denied

    and it will be,

        the mania begins.

With every plea,

    with each entreaty,

        the supply becomes
more scarce

            the cost
        soars higher

            the
        craving more
        palpable

until you at last succumb to the withdrawal,

    perish,

        or survive in a cold
turkey coma

while the pusher finds a new user

    and you search the streets
for a fresh source.

The Late Bloomer

Dazzling in the dewy mist
perched high on the tallest limb
      the last bloom of the gardenia
          shines in the evening sun.
It fills the air with its perfume,
      enticing passers by
          to stop and embrace the moment,
              before it disappears.
Behold the majesty of the late bloomer,
waiting until the waning of the season
      to display its most gorgeous petals
          and unleash its allure.
It has held tightly to its life force
bursting into brilliance
      with little regard for convention.
The late bloomer cares not
that it is the last to fulfill its glory,
      it revels in the light upon its being
          and basks in the spotlight,
              revealing its beauty to the universe.
The late bloomer lives in its moment
and faces the coming winter with joy and resolve
      knowing that the long-awaited bud
          of perseverance and promise
              has blossomed at last.

Corona

Humanity is such a presumptive species.
We assume that we have dominion of life on our planet,
but every so often Nature takes us down a peg
and gives us a Satori slap.
Nature is the Sensei
and we are just the Soto plebes,
novices of life and learning
and must be shown the correct path.
We think we know of life
but we are just as unenlightened
as the viruses that seek our demise.
Yet, we persist in our obsession
that we are in control
and have power over other life.
Wake up people
and learn to coexist
all life is relevant
what matters is how we interact with it
and each other.
Respect all life.
Learn to combat infirmity,
and for God's sake wash your damn hands.

The Warm Light of Normalcy

The wisteria had just started to bloom.
The first buds of the trees
    cracked through their winter seed husks,
        as the vernal equinox
            turned the seasons.
It was then the cloud covered the sun,
    and made the rainbows fade away.
We hid from the storm,
    like an ostrich with our heads in the sand,
      but our beings were still exposed to the peril.
As the tempest took its toll,
    we cowered in isolation,
        afraid that our fate was to be decided by the devil,
            who had destroyed our defensive shield,
                in a fit of greed filled political lunacy.
But the sky was still filled with light,
    the glow of angels
        that selflessly served mankind,
            and resurrected hope.

Each wave of devastation
>   is met with a levee of prayer,
>   and a bastion of caring and courage,
>   as we battle our demons from without and within
>   and seek a new beginning,
>   in the warm light of normalcy.

The Wren

Ah my diminutive friend,
    the wren.
Warbling and chirping,
    flitting across the sunrise,
        your song in harmony
           with the chimes in the wind
           and with the music of the earth's turning.
Your stature belies your courage,
    as you are assailed by those that mock your song.
You defend your nest with unrelenting spirit
    and woe to those who misjudge your
determination.
I envy you my friend,
    the undaunted wren.
You face each moment with a song in your heart
    and the courage of a classic hero.
You cast your fears into the breeze
    and live life as full and free as the sky in which
you fly.
How I envy thee,
    my diminutive friend, the wren.

The Wilted Rose

Though the edges of the blooms are withered and sere,
the leaves wrinkled,
the stems dry, cracked and stiff,
The wilted rose is still glorious,
regaled in beauty and splendor
shining in the light of each new day.

Living

I live for hope

I hope for life

I struggle to understand

but understand the struggle

I am lost in the love of art

yet lose at the art of love

I try to answer the question

I always question the answer

I accept the challenge

and still challenge the accepted

I wait for the dream of redemption

and dream for the redemption of the wait.

Wonder Why

I'm not long for this world
        but I'm not sure about another one.
Some say you can live forever,
        some say when you're done,
you're just done.
Life is filled with so much wonder and magic,
        it makes me believe there must be more.
So, when I enter the hall of mirrors,
        I just hope
                I pick the right door.

Life is a rolling highway
        you dodge traffic from lane to lane
                some days the ride is easy
                      some days are jammed with pain.
Its hard to see the mile post
        when the sky is pouring rain.
                I just pray I can find my way
                      if I must pass this way again.

The world keeps on turning
        time keeps passing by,
                passion keeps burning,
                      the smoke makes lovers cry.

> But the fires of love and life
>   we know will someday die,
>   and I just sit and sing
>   and wonder why
>
>   and wonder why
> I just sit and sing
>   and wonder why.

The Night of the Pearl

I first met Belle Fox-Martin at the Black Pearl. She was hanging out with the irrepressible Leppy McCarthy and I adored them both.

She liked my songs.

She had the unique presence and style of elite sophistication and reminded me of Audrey Hepburn. She was gorgeous and talented and amazingly, seemed to like me, so much so, that she financed my first recording and gave me a wonderful zircon encrusted airplane pin that I wore religiously, until I lost it somehow in the move back to the south.

I cried when I couldn't find it.

So, with Belle's kind gifts in hand I was off to Boston, to Renaissance Studios for the first effort of "High Flying Bird".

It was a painful and excruciating experience, the engineer did not share my vision for the tune and a huge chunk of time was wasted trying to get the perfect tone from a set of Claves. Luckily, Biggie Korn, stepped in and salvaged the session. Eric Sampson nailed a virtuoso flute performance in one take and I had a record.

My friend Tom Pacheco had recently signed with Fox music and he set up a meeting for me with Ray Fox in New York City and we were off.

Little did I know, that I was in for a life altering experience.

Through the good fortune of meeting and subsequently performing with the exquisite banjoist, Roger Sprung I was able to be a part of the Newport Folk Festival in 1969 and became an acquaintance of Danny Kalb, the guitarist from The Blues Project. He and his beautiful and enigmatic girlfriend, Lyndall Erb crashed at my place a few nights for the event and Danny offered to put me up when I was in New York.

So after the session, with demo in hand, Tom and I headed for the Big Apple.

Ray Fox had an office like a cavern, if his idea was to awe and impress it worked. I played him my demo and he listened intently and after it finished, he made the most prophetic and revealing statements I had ever heard.

"Marv you got a real good sound going there I like it," he said, and I was on the edge of my chair. "here's what I want you to do, go home and lose 30 pounds and come back and see me." What! I was livid, he said it was good, that I had a sound, wasn't that all that mattered? He looked me straight in the eye and said these words that are forever etched in my psyche, "Marv if you give me a great sound and no look, I can't sell it, but give me an ok sound and a great look and I can make you a star." It hit like a hammer. I wasn't obese I only weighed about 165 back then and being young and full of piss and vinegar and myself, rose and stormed out of his office and my dreams of pop stardom were over.

After the demo debacle, we headed down to the Village to Danny's apartment and I found out that the Fates weren't done with me yet and I was going to get schooled in what the scene was all about.

I knocked on the door at #3 Bowery Street and Lyndall answered, she was a striking vision, worldly and confident with that aura of celebrity about her. She was with two of her girlfriends and they were smoking a bunch of hash and invited us in. She said that Danny was on Long Island playing a gig at Your Fathers Mustache, a popular music venue of the day, but we were welcome to crash.

After a massive consumption of hashish, one of her friends suggested they go get a bite, and we all headed through the Village streets to find a restaurant. All of a sudden, on the other side of the street I saw two guys I recognized immediately, Jimmy Carl Black and Frank Zappa and they saw Lyndall and crossed over to us. It was quite obvious that these were quite good buddies of Lyndall's, their embrace was the kind that spoke of carnal knowledge, either in the past or future. Pleasantries were exchanged and we were again on our way. This was the point where my mind and reality started separating, but I was enjoying the journey so far, and trucked on.

We ended up at a place called The Cookery, on Bleeker St. and we sat at a table on the patio, you could see all the way down Bleeker into Washington Square from our vantage point. Without warning the Fates unleashed a sobering lesson, entering and taking the table next to us were two, dare I say it, Rock Idols, Charlie Watts and Mick Jagger. They sat, nodded in recognition to Lyndall and ordered drinks and a nosh. We had done the same.

As we supped, you could see in the Square that a young hippie fellow, I'm guessing 13 or 14 years old, had a squirrel on a string like a pet, and was delighting the crowd of hipsters that were gathered in the park on a pleasant late afternoon summer's day. A commotion ensued as the squirrel got away from the lad and scurried up a tree and the insuppressible youngster climbed up after it.

Enter stage left, a mounted city cop who was telling the kid to get down. The young man persisted after his pet and the officer reached up grabbed him by the ankle and pulled him from the tree to the ground. All hell broke loose, the crowd erupted, pulled the officer off his steed and started pummeling him. In seconds, a force of cops in riot gear descended on the crowd and the battle ensued. It was a full-scale riot and it was slowly working its way up Bleeker toward us. I glanced over at the other table and noticed that Jagger was rapt by the scene and furiously making notes on a small pocket pad. I don't think it's any coincidence that a year later The Stones released a track called "Heartbreaker," the inspiration was blatant.

At this point one of Lyndall's friends blasely said, "This is boring, let's go uptown".

She hailed a cab and we were off.

I had never been to Max's Kansas City before and wasn't quite sure what to make of it. It had two rooms, a downstairs bar and an upstairs showroom, we went in the bar which to my surprise had swinging doors and was painted entirely black, entirely, everything was black except for a red neon tube that ran the length of the walls and was the only light source. The place was empty except for a booth in the very back where Lou and most of the Velvet Underground were huddled together, it was like six or seven people in one booth, but I couldn't help but recognize Nico.

We took a booth and the girls ordered drinks, Tom and I had no cash, so we just sat.

Then it happened. The swinging doors burst open and in waltzed the queen. Janis was dressed in gig regalia and had Peter Coyote on one arm and a guy I recognized from Rolling Stone as one of the head Diggers, they sauntered in, then Janis saw Lyndall and she shed both guys and came and plopped down in the booth next to Lyndall right across from me. They hugged and started chattering like only two old roommates could. The waiter came over and asked Janis if she wanted a drink. Janis stated that she wanted a pitcher of Sangria. The waiter looked at Tom and I and said how many glasses do you want and Janis said with a look that could emasculate and strip the hide from a grizzly bear said, " I said I'll have a pitcher of Sangria." The waiter brought it and Janis drank it like a mug of beer.

She began catching up with Lyndall, they talked about the scene and about ongoing projects. That's when Janis said she was through with Big Brother, Kosmic, and Full Tilt, and was putting together a group to go to L.A. to record and she had everyone she needed except a bass player and even though she knew I played guitar, Lyndall had only ever seen me perform as a bassist. That's when she started kicking me under the table, she kicked hard and she wore western boots with a little silver toe cap, but I couldn't speak, even if I tried to no words would have come out. To use the cliché phrase, my mind was blown, I was nearly comatose. I could hear and see and understand, but I was frozen, and Lyndall kicked even harder. I was starting to bleed.

Janis finished off the Sangria and said she was off to Fillmore East and as suddenly as she had entered the Texas tornado stormed out the door. The silence was palpable, and Lyndall said, let's go to the apartment. We did, her friends hooked up with Coyote and the Digger and had taken the bed and the couch so Tom and I laid on the floor and as I was about to slumber off amid the moans and squeaks of hashish driven coitus around me, Lyndall bent over and whispered in my ear, " You had your chanc.e"

The next morning I awoke before anyone else, left and made my way to the Port Authority and took a bus to my home in Lorton, Virginia. I sat in the field across from our house for two days, watched the clouds, listened to the birds and gathered my sanity, wondering what the Fates had in store for me next. In retrospect, I have thought long and hard about the events of that evening, and have come to firmly believe that the reason for my silence was that my guardian angels were sitting on my shoulder with their hands over my mouth. If I had gone down that road to L.A. with Janis, I am pretty sure they would have found me lying beside her dead like her just a month later.

Belle Star

She gives me
hope,
and the faith
to believe,
that all my
trials will
soon be
relieved.
The way she
takes the
time,
to find out
who you
really are
pretends she
is just the
sunset,
when in fact
she is the
morning
star.

Carolina Lady

Gaunt jawed and lean,
denim and lace
ragged,
but clean as new rain.
Hard as nails,
soft as cotton
name you can't remember,
face cannot be forgotten.
Red clay
molded into a soul,
washed in the flood,
and risen,
in the new spring grass.
Telling tales of loves remembered,
prophecies
of times yet to pass.

Genesis

Soft at first,
like the trickle of light evening rain
gliding down the white satin face
of gardenias
at your door.
My love for you grew,
a small reflective pool
dappled with drops of passion,
till overflowing,
unable to be contained,
it splashed,
racing down
the mountain of my soul.
A light dancing brook,
of unrestrained
flowing adoration,
growing deeper
wider
with every moment,
every kiss,
every touch.
Then suddenly a stream,
a flood of admiration
with a current of desire
so strong
it could not be denied,
never turned back,
its flows ever onward growing

more and more
till at last,
the tide of love
has risen past the peaks of my body and mind.
An ocean of longing
in which I am consumed,
given totally to the life liquid,
flowing between us
around us
and over us.

I see you now,
riding on the crest of love, rocking in its storms,
swaying to its lullabies
and I wonder,
will you ever cast your ship aside,
and slip into the warm beckoning depths,
float with the tide, letting its gently touch engulf
you?

Or will you shun the ocean,
for fear of drowning
and sail your ship to other ports.

I know there will be other sailors,
to tell you tales of passion and delight,
to show you pleasures,
fulfill your dreams,
give you gifts of grace and beauty.
But there will never be, never exist,
that will hold you in more esteem,
see in you more beauty,
admire more in your spirit,
or feel for you more desire,
than this,
the sea who loves you.

Disco Nights

Satin and leather
slick and rough
slide across the floor and strut your stuff.
Just can't seem to get enough.
You want it.
Jive!
Shuck!
Those soft, clean hands
faces in oily muck.

Don Pablo's

Lurking at Don Pablo's
to hear the gypsies, sing.
Waiting for the magic
those melodies will bring.
In the dregs of winter
you feel a touch of spring
and like some newborn bluebird,
you begin to sing,
out loud!

Desire

Standing on the edge of oblivion,
peering over the precipice,
teetering,
trying to find a balance in life.
Seeking solace
and perspective
in a precarious world.
Suddenly,
Destiny dances into proximity
doing the electric slide
and I am tempted
to boot scoot boogie
into a new dimension,
abandon the search for salvation
and yield to the night's
carnal ambiguity.
But she already has a companion
and alas,
I am all too comfortable
with my own delusions.

Five Points

Her demeanor was perfection.
She glided across the floor
in barely there sandals
and her breasts
according to the standards of décolletage were
exemplary,
but alas,
she didn't know who Yeats was
not to mention Ferlinghetti
so, sayonara my princess.

Grass

Night draws close,
    the nervous edges of uncertainty
        that circles my existence.
As the dusk falls,
    my strengths fades.
      I lay limp,
        wet with dew,
   waiting to feel once again,
      the warm white light.
Drawing me closer
   to the source.
      My nourishment!

Java Jive

I sat sipping coffee,

lost in the urban jungle,

enraptured by the passing wildlife,

when I first noticed her presence.

She had shoes like a Greek goddess

but her demeanor was more Amazon queen.

Although the arrows she fired at me were merely visual,

they hit their mark

and I bled and retreated in haste

to the safety of my still steaming cup.

Tuning Up

Sounds of sallow light,
    crash through reverberations.
I bend
    to touch you
        and bring you closer to the harmony
            around us.
    You flash!
    Passion
        singes the edge of my eyes,
            and leaves me stranded.

Sittin' In

Little deaths.

Trying to catch the moment,

    and make it last.

    No applause.

The long walk back to the table,

those endless seconds waiting for approval.

    Was it good?

        Did it make it?

            If it felt good, then it was.

Reconciling yourself you take your place,

    back among the nameless faces.

You could feel something,

    or could you feel at all?

But now the backbeat boogie

and the backside slide

    pull you away,

        steal your mind.

            Nothing to feel anyway.

Christmas With Harry

I wonder.
What prompted you to take pen in hand,
    make commitments,
    from your soul
    in black and white.
I wonder,
about myself.
    What was evoked,
    what was choked?

I scaled the mountain,
    to find the solace
    of the snow and pine cathedral,
    to find the union
    of mind and space.
Found that solace,
    The solstice
    The human race

Ol' Van Herder would agree,
    further into life
    not behind,
    not the child,
    but now
    alive and free!

Then suddenly,
> I am the gypsy,
> I am Don Pablo,
> I am not beneath the wheel,
> I am not a cog.

The Time Before Knowing

In the time before knowing
    there were dreams,
episodes of soaring in flight
    and running with tigers.
Schemes of existence and propagation
    did not exist.
Life flowed seamlessly,
    uninterrupted by thought.
Laughter was ever present,
    and tears were only shed from physical pain.
Before awareness,
    of myself or humanity,
        there was only living,
            and living was matter of fact.
And now,
    in the decline of years,
I seek to return to those days of unenlightened
    bliss.
Dip my toes in the creek
    and wade up to my neck unafraid.

I want to grasp and hold every emotion,
    cling to every experience as if it were brand new,
        for I fear the loss of them.
I often think of those days,
    spent running through the fields of hay,
        feeling the wind on my face,
            the smell of new turned earth,
  the sun warming my shoulders,
      oblivious to the world beyond my being,
        and ponder knowledge.
Would we be better off
    if we never bit the "apple"?
        or are we now just
           foolish
and frightened to be our true selves.

Under the Watchful Eye of Venus

I sat under the watchful eye of Venus
    as the carnival swarmed around me.
Clowns in sequins and glitter
    and geniuses in Cargo shorts
        danced and pranced,
            with pinup fiddle players
        frolicking on the shores of the swamp.
Guitars twanged long into the night,
    as slender maidens danced to different drummers.
I caught her casting a glance at me,
    we spoke and looked each other in the eye,
        and for a moment it was all too real.
I called her sweetheart,
    and she feigned disdain, but smiled knowingly,
        and I longed to know her secrets,
    but she wasn't ready to tell a stranger the truth.
But still we shared a moment,
    as the universe swirled around us
under the watchful eye of Venus.

Sojouners

Sojourners
    carrying their life in a backpack
        stare at my trappings and smirk.
Their legs,
    weary with treading the hard road,
their hearts
    heavy with the baggage they tote,
their minds
    filled with poetry to quote.
I wonder what they think of the songs that I sing
and if moved, would they dance,
    shed their togs and clogs and prance,
        in the languid moonlight.
Forget their destination,
    lay down the quest,
        and revel in the moment.
But they just keep walking,
    wearing a wry smile
        continue the endless journey,
            down the hard road mile.

The Chosen Ones?

Other beings
    are confounded by our existence.
We thrive against all odds
    and promulgate at an astounding rate.
We are an infestation of humanity,
    that worries other life forms.
Not quite pests,
    but an invasive species none the less.
Tolerated,
    but in need of control.
Yet, we continue to profess our overwhelming
    need to inhabit all the universe
    and expound the belief that we are omnipotent,
but we struggle with the insignificance of our being.
When faced with our own shortcomings,
    we fawn in the face of dilemma
        and rage at the unknown for relief.
Is it any wonder that we refuse to acknowledge?
    that we are at the bottom of the pecking order
        in the celestial lineage,
        but espouse that we are the chosen ones?
The question of course is who does the choosing.

Free Tickets

By 1965, the Folk Festival had outgrown the Casino and George Wein finagled moving it to a field in Miantonomi Park across the road from a corn field. It has disappeared now and is the home of a highway, a motel and a shopping center, more proof that life is temporal.

It was a beautiful day and I had taken leave all weekend, I was in the Navy then, going to Class A Storekeeper school at Fleet Training Center.

If you were into the music and especially if you played, the afternoon workshops were where the action was and a good size crowd of us had gathered at the entrance gate to run and get close to the acts we wanted to see and hear. Suddenly, like a heraldic angel arriving from heaven surrounded by a mystic aura, the throng was stunned to see the goddess herself, Joan Baez walk up to the gate. In her hand she held the tickets to every box seat for that evening's performances and with a sly grin, tossed them into crowd of screaming guitar and banjo pickers and gayly skipped away with her entourage. The magic and madness had begun, and my ship was about to sail on uncharted seas.

So that night when Bob shocked the world with a Stratocaster, and more to my liking Mike Bloomfield debuted with Paul Butterfield, I sat munching popcorn, drinking a beer and sharing the dude next to me's weed, and reveling in all the Folk Music world had to offer.

    The next morning, I awoke in a small copse lying on a pile of pine needles with a rabbit less than two inches from my nose starring into my blood shot eyes. We exchanged greetings, and each hopped away to search for the next adventure. Perhaps Alice wasn't so fictional after all.

Spirits Of Samhain

Death watch,
      Sightings of floating freedoms.
          Spirits alive
              on islands
                  stranded.
Silently
    I wait,
Until my desire can no longer be restrained.
My presence does not disturb you,
      as long as I am neatly hung
          in your closet,
              skeletal remains of dying passions.
But if my spirit rises
      shakes my bones
          in pursuit of true release,
You shut the door
      and whisper among yourselves
          that you never really experienced
              anything.
Truth is so haunting.

Road Dreams

I was riding
the night train,
      to Memphis.
Jamming
with the rhythm
      of the rain
         on the windowpane.
Stuck out on the road again,
with only one shoe
and had to walk,
barefoot
      across the stage.

Morning Prayer

First light of the day
     warm my heart.
First wave of the new tide
     wash my soul.
First breeze of Earth's new turning
     cool my burning soul.
Out of the black night
     I rise,
          Weary,
     pray for new awakening,
          rejoice in new beginning,
              and give thanks,
for one more try.

Driving Through Georgia

The wisteria strangles the redbud
    as they sprawl across the red dirt.
The resplendent drama of the equinox
    erupts across the landscape
        as the renewal of life returns.
Drowsy beings emerge from cold slumbers,
    stretch and feel the sap swelling in their veins.
But I am racing down the highway of existence
    too fast
        and cannot stop
            to dive into the ocean of color
    and swim on the rising tide,
        only mental photographs will have to
    suffice for memories.
Time has become my most precious commodity in
my meager portfolio
    and I have spent too much
        with no return.

Seven

On seven shores of the seven seas
        seven sailors will fall on their knees,
                to thank the seven winds that blew
                        the seven sails that sailed true.
Beneath the seven stars that shine
        with light to guide seven souls divine,
                the seven worlds will at last unite
                        when seven loves come into sight.

Perspective

I was trying to write between the lines
with a blunt crayon
when I suddenly arrived at the give a shit point.
Wondering if it was worth the effort,
I remember art is all about
perspective
I sit in the café sipping wine
I watch a lovely derriere sashay by
and realize that I am more transfixed by the sway of
the drape
rather than the jounce of the flesh.
Is it age or refinement that has changed my interest?
As we talk, I gather the courage to stare
deep into your eyes
and see that your vision is not clouded by fear or
trepidation
your smile is genuine and embracing
and I long to be closer to your presence.
You say that you have a penchant for pajamas as
clothing
while lying on your daybed beneath the swaying
palms.
I imagine the undulation of the drape on your thighs
and take another sip.
You willingly take my hand as we walk
and I want to swing your body to mine
and press my lips against yours
but I dare not.

Your perspective
may not applaud the passion play
and I am not willing to gamble at losing your presence
so newly discovered.
I dream of further exploration,
perhaps in pajamas beneath the palms,
bid you goodnight
and drive on to find a new perspective.

Politic

The Princeps of pliancy parades across the promenade
never expecting to encounter
the barriers of dogmatic determination
that stand in the face of truth.

The uncommon sense of defiance they exude

hardens the malleability of his persona,

forces him to dig deep into his foundations

to withstand the diatribes of destruction

thrown at his constructs.

This onslaught of malfeasance

only stiffens the erection of his resolve

and forces him to push against the unrelenting.

Tete a tete ensues

and forgiveness is lost.

Priorities

It's all a matter of priorities.
    I remember my father
        yelling at me in a fit of frustration,
            "you better get your priorities straight."
I didn't understand at the time,
    were they bent or misaligned?
        I realize now,
           that maybe they were,
                at least according to my father's
        definition.
I have come to learn
    that priorities govern the decisions we make in life,
        the relevance of objectivity,
           the importance of being,
                what matters most.
But priorities are governed by the status
    of one's existence.
True, the basic needs of life are the same for all
    but circumstance
        often decides the priority
What matters most?
    Survival,
        love,
           art,
                what are your priorities,
                    are they straight?

Have you decided which path your journey should take?
    or are you lost,
        hesitant,
            unable to decide,
                what matters most?
Inevitably we must opt for the road
    that fulfills our hopes,
        dreams
            and desires.
                and pray we take the correct
                    doorway.
In the end
    it's all a matter of priorities.

Lady Bug

Oh, my little Lady Bug,
where did you come from?
Did you fly in
or perhaps, hitch a ride
on an unaware host,
who cut foliage at Penland studio,
in search of a warmer clime?
Oh, my little Lady Bug,
how did you end up in this wine glass?
Did you think this liquid could relieve your thirst?
Were you just swimming,
trying to stay afloat,
or maybe you desired a sip
and decided to take an intoxicating plunge,
risking doom to indulge in a taste of forbidden fruit?
But alas, you have survived and seem to be reveling in
your vineyard fantasy now,
as you stagger across the table
reeling and dodging the cards and chips
of the game being dealt.
Oh, my little Lady Bug,
have you forgotten how to fly?
You could simply spread your wings
and find a haven
from the peril that surrounds you,
but you linger and risk all.
Is it an indelible memory, or the taste of danger on your lips
that holds you here,

or are you just overwhelmed in the moment?
Courage in the face of precarious fate
may be your undoing.
Oh, my little Lady Bug
Come and rest in my hand
and let me carry you to a safe landing
away from dangers unknown
where you can live and thrive
until your next encounter with
the juice of the grape.
Oh, my little Lady Bug.

Hazelnut Dream

It was the kind of damp, cold night
that insulated and isolated us
and made it seem we were the only two people in the world.
Searching for a refuge from the rain,
We stopped in at a quaint Gelateria,
she said she had a craving for Hazelnut.
We sat and shared a cup.
I was transfixed as I watched her tongue
dance on the small plastic spoon
as she savored the taste of the creamy treat.
Licking slowly,
then darting enticingly across the spoon.
Closing her lips to make the taste linger in her mouth.
Suddenly, my loins erupted,
as I imagined
the head of my cock was the spoon,
covered in hazelnut cream and her saliva,
her seductive tongue lingering on its tip.
Her lips closing tight
and sucking the spoon dry.
She asked "what was wrong"
as my eyes rolled back into my head,
"Aren't you enjoying the Gelato"?
I assured her I was enthralled with it
and asked if she would like some more.
I knew I certainly would!

Diver

In the same breath,
        she is my siren and my lighthouse.
Her beauty and wit enchant me
        and I am drawn to be by her side.
Forsaking all others, the pleasure of her presence pervades my senses.
I am adrift in a sea of devotion, not looking for any rescue.
        I dream of diving deep into her soul,
        never to surface again,
        awash in eternal bliss.
And at the same moment,
        her charm and intelligence guide me
        across troubled waters
        as we navigate life's mysteries and sail in our hearts' harmony.
She is a beacon for my desire
        The light of her smile
        shines through the darkness of doubt
        quells the fear of misgiving
        and soothes and satisfies my soul
        her aura is that of an Angel
        gleaming through the firmament
and as she touches my hand, I am ready to leap
and lose my being
        deep in an ocean of love.

Rebirth

Her kiss awoke me from my long, dreary winters sleep,
    and I was reborn into a summer's dream,
I had long forgotten,
    wiped the stale sand from my eyes,
and I once again could see the light and beauty of life.
    I trembled with excitement,
        but felt the ease of perfection,
            the fit of comfort,
  that only comes with love.
When she touched my hand, the world stopped turning,
    and the loss of emotional gravity
        sent my heart soaring through the universe,
    and I was lost in the wonder of new tomorrows.
Destiny washes over life with a slow river current
    sometimes barely producing a ripple or wave
        but is constantly moving and changing,
redirecting the course of existence when least expected.
Suddenly I beheld a fresh destination,
    and was able to stop swimming against the tide,
    and float effortlessly
        to a new haven of bliss.
I now am ecstatic,
    with the revelation of the loss of longing
      and full of trepidation
            at the new beginnings
but trust in the truth of friendship, partnership, and love.

Fine Art

Sculpted beauty,
      a goddess statuesque, reclining on the sofa
      my precious odalisque.
A living work of art,
      a feast for the eye, I crave to devour you
      but hear your reluctant sigh.
So, I will just sup upon your vision,
      worship you from my chair.
Savor your countenance
      like a fine wine
            and cherish your presence there.

Missing You

Your touch
    transforms my being
        and I am lost
            wandering across
                unknown landscapes,
                    hoping to behold your visage.
Longing does little
    to describe the depth
        of my emotion
and only your kiss
    can quell the anxiety of the separation.

The Wait

The cool solitude of the pillow
    I cradle in your absence is little compensation
        for the warmth of your heart and soul,
            that I crave to embrace.
I dream of my lips lingering on yours
    and feeling your breath engulfing my being.
As I lay alone
I count the hours, minutes, seconds until once again,
    I can feel your body next to mine
        and hear your sweet soft laughter in my ears.
I rise, pace, drink, and return to the barren sheets,
    sprawl on the linen,
        close my eyes, so I can see your smile
            and await your return.

Just Because

Because I can still feel the wind blowing in my hair,
    I know I am alive.
Because the sun fills my eyes with shining light,
    I know there is hope.
Because I can hear your laughter,
    I know there is joy.
Because I can feel your hand on my face,
    I know there is passion.
Because your heart and mind are touching my soul,
    I know there is love.

Rainbow Time

As we held each other,
surrounded by rainbows
I suckled her breast like a child
and stroked the marks
on her supple hips
left by the birthing
and realized the
power and strength
in the fortitude of femininity.
More than perseverance,
she embraces her life
and its travails
making it her magic,
casting the spell of her beautiful countenance
on any who are fortunate enough
to behold her presence.
Her resilience to love in the face of
trauma and despair inspires me
and makes me desire her even more.
I am awed by the majesty of her presence
and overwhelmed at the providence to be in her arms.

Love

As she basked in the crisp autumn sun at the fountain
>her hand caressed the water,

A transcendent serenity enveloped her being.
>I felt my heart leave my body,
>>and beg to reside with hers.

With a wry smile and a gentle touch,
>she accepted the request.
>Two hearts entwined,
>>and our eyes locked together on a new tomorrow.

Beyond Shangri-La

It was astonishing
     how in one night the two bare wires of our souls
touched, sparked, and ignited
         into a blaze of passion
             that burns hotter than the sun.
Now, basking in the warmth of that explosion,
     I watch her dance
         with the shadows of her hands
            on the ceiling
               projected by the light of the salt lamp.
Her body glows in the pink light radiating a sensuality
beyond mortal being.
     She has an angelic aura
         that consumes my soul.
I kiss her lips hard.
     Her eyes widen revealing oceans of a netherworld,
unexplored, vast and deep
         and I am enraptured.
We clasp hands and she leads me to new experiences of
profound ecstasy,
     on our journey beyond Shangri-La.

Alone Together

We walked alone, together
    along the shore
        communing with Mother Ocean,
    loving her
        and each other.
Sublime in the serenity
    of our own thoughts and feelings,
        yet sharing more of each other's soul
            with one another than if we were
    conjoined.
    No purpose,
        no destination,
            just nature
                and each other's love.
I watched her feet leave tiny impressions in the sand
    before the tide erased them
        and saw she was walking on her toes
            in ballet with the sea.
    Skittering through the foam with the sandpipers
        giggling with ecstasy
and for a moment, the world stopped
    as the opera of Poseidon encored,
        the waves in basso,
            the birds in soprano aria.
I was at peace
    in this place
        surrounded by beauty, magic and love
            and could want for nothing more in
    life.

www.ingramcontent.com/pod-product-compliance
Lightning Source LLC
Chambersburg PA
CBHW041131110526
44592CB00020B/2773